MW00851447

Call Me Maybe, Home & More Hot Singles

ISBN 978-1-4803-5268-1

HAL•LEONARD®
CORPORATION
7777 W. BLUEMOUND RD. P.O. BOX 13819 MILWAUKEE, WI 53213

Visit Hal Leonard Online at
www.halleonard.com

Contents

CALL ME MAYBE

Words and Music by CARLY RAE JEPSEN,
JOSHUA RAMSAY and TAVISH CROWE

Moderate Pop

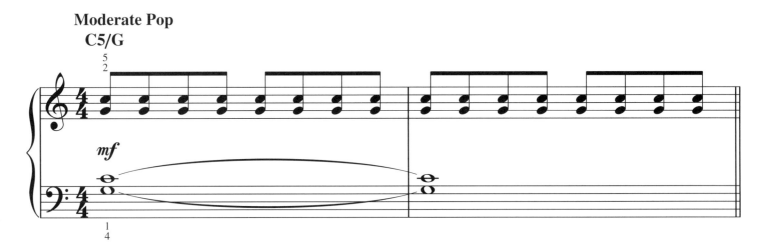

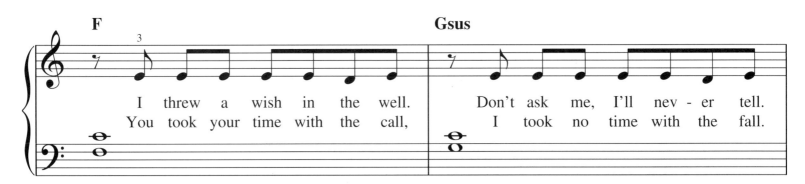

I threw a wish in the well.
You took your time with the call,

Don't ask me, I'll nev - er tell.
I took no time with the fall.

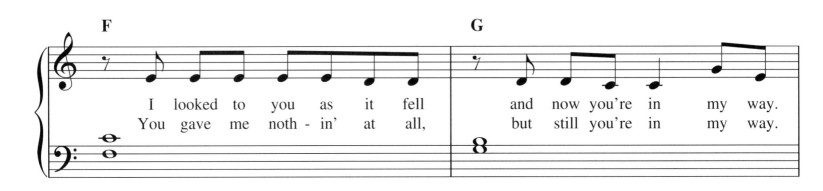

I looked to you as it fell
You gave me noth - in' at all,

and now you're in my way.
but still you're in my way.

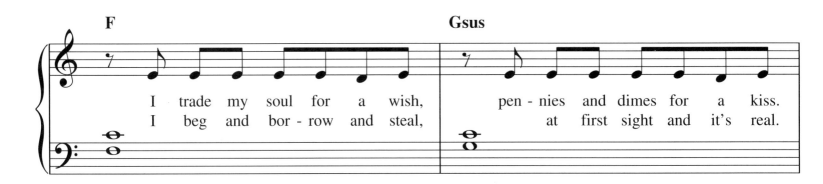

I trade my soul for a wish,
I beg and bor - row and steal,

pen - nies and dimes for a kiss.
at first sight and it's real.

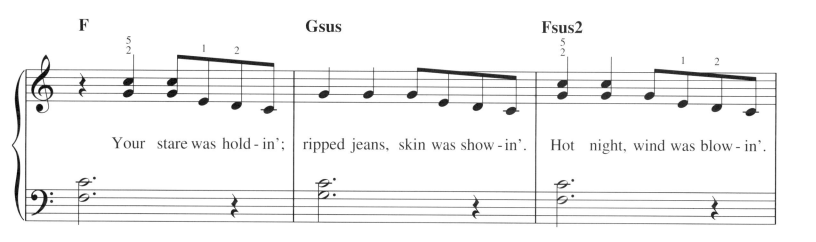

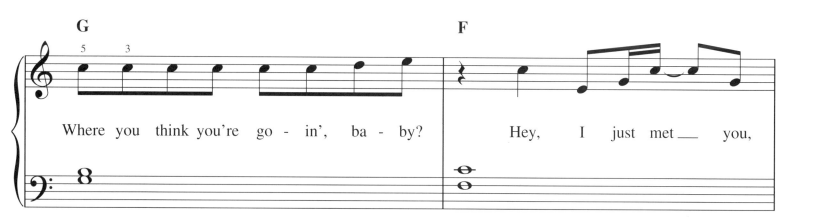

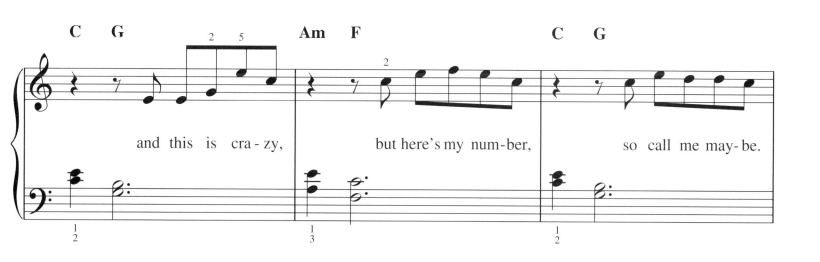

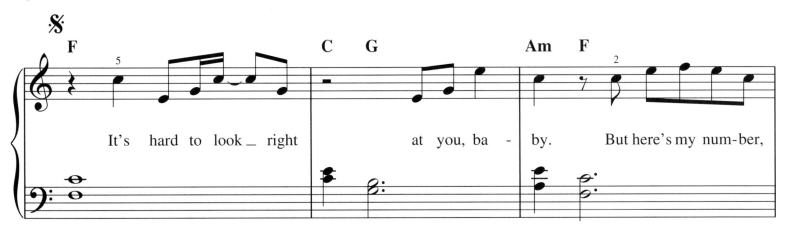

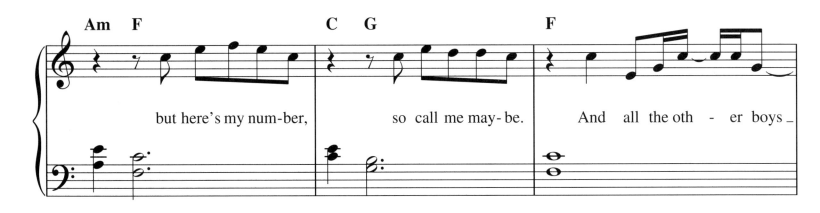

7

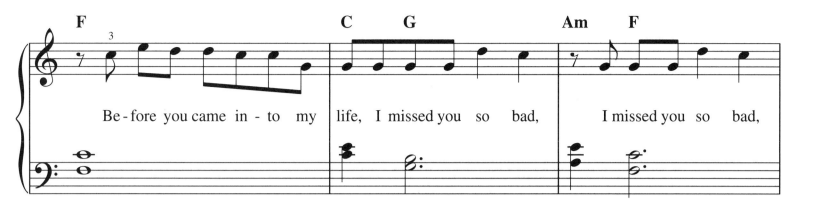

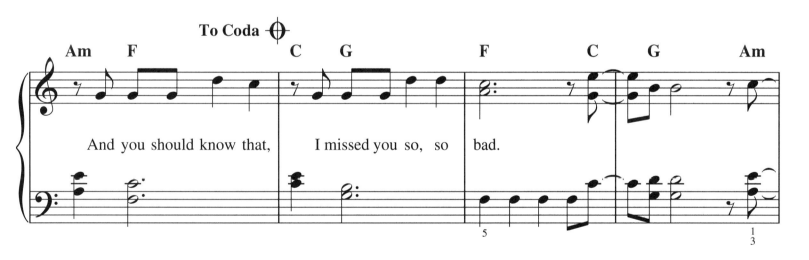

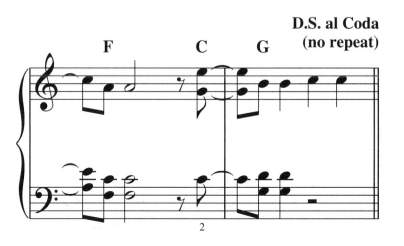

HEART ATTACK

Words and Music by JASON EVIGAN,
MITCH ALLAN, SEAN DOUGLAS,
NIKKI WILLIAMS, AARON PHILLIPS
and DEMI LOVATO

Put-tin' my de-fen-ses up 'cause I don't wan-na fall in love. If I

ev-er did that, I think I'd have a heart at - tack.

Nev-er put my love out on the line. Nev - er said yes to the right guy.
Nev-er break a sweat for oth-er guys. When you come a-round I get par-a-lyzed.

Nev-er had trou-ble get-ting what I want but when it comes to you, I'm nev-er good e -
Ev-'ry time I try to be my-self, it comes out wrong like a cry for

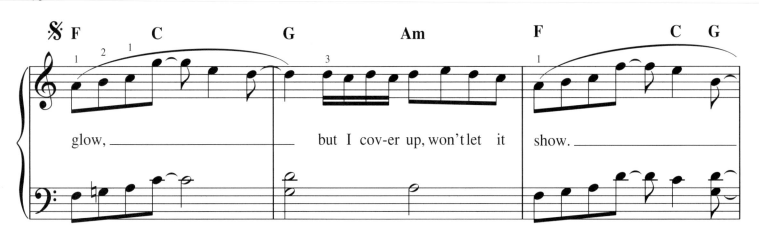

glow, _____ but I cov-er up, won't let it show. _____

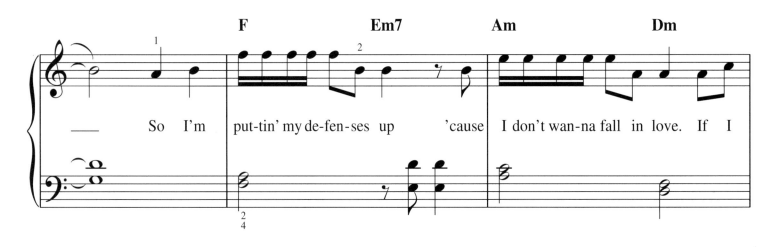

_____ So I'm put-tin' my de-fen-ses up 'cause I don't wan-na fall in love. If I

To Coda ⊕

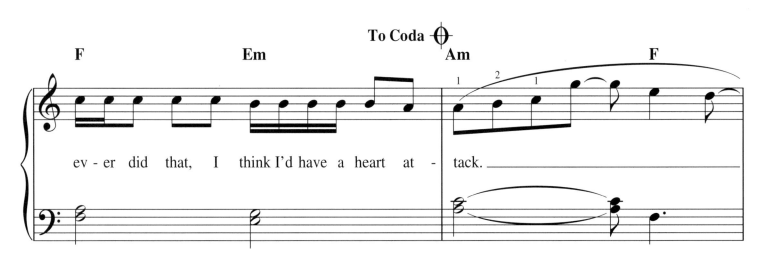

ev - er did that, I think I'd have a heart at - tack. _____

1.

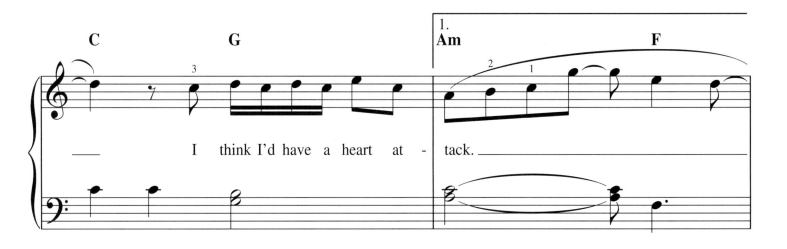

_____ I think I'd have a heart at - tack. _____

I think I'd have a heart at - tack. _____ tack. _____

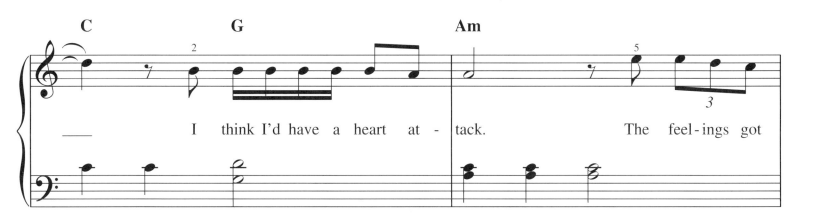

I think I'd have a heart at - tack. _____ The feel-ings got

lost in my lungs. They're burn-ing, I'd rath-er be numb and there's no one else to blame. _____

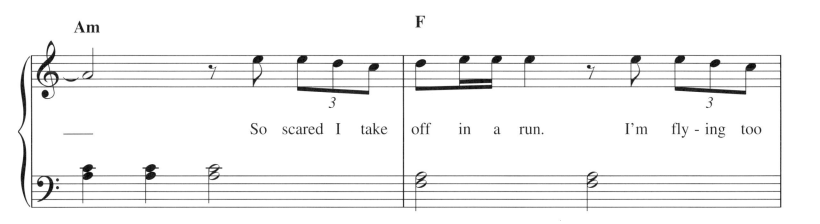

_____ So scared I take off in a run. I'm fly-ing too

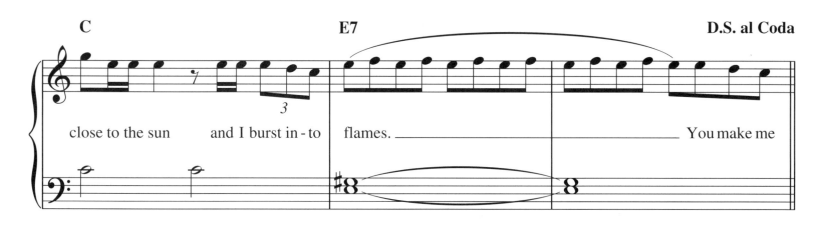

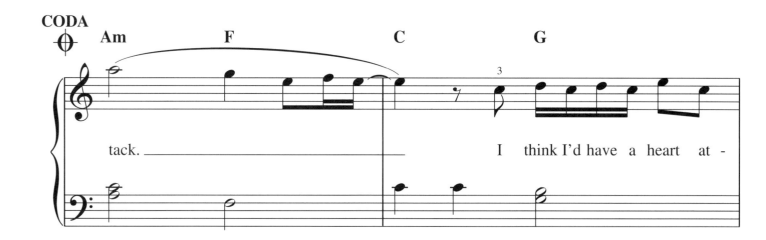

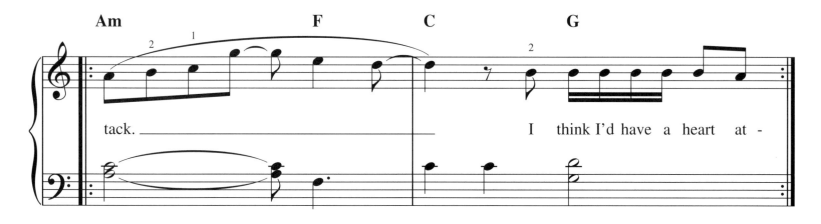

HOME

Words and Music by GREG HOLDEN
and DREW PEARSON

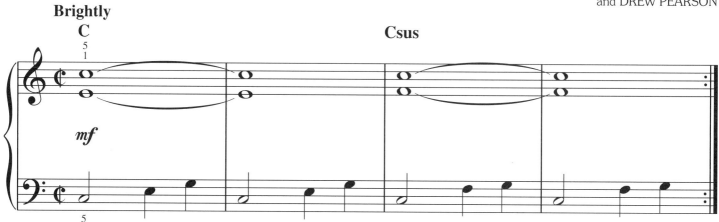

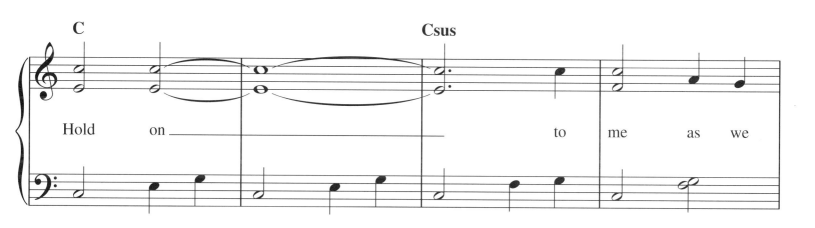

Hold   on   to   me   as   we

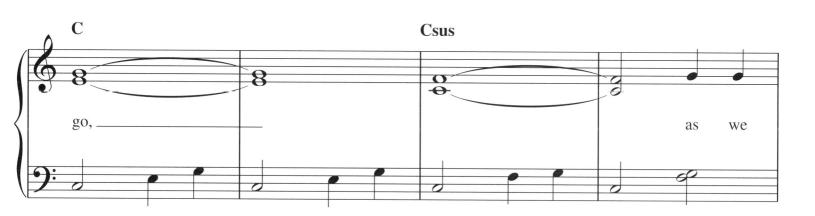

go,   as   we

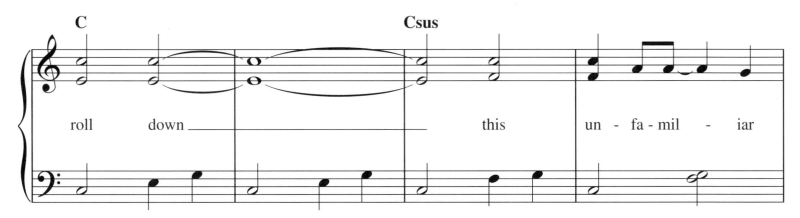

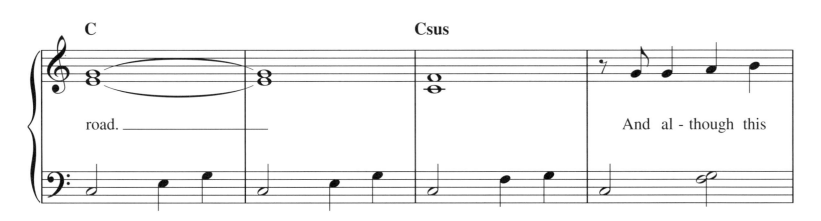

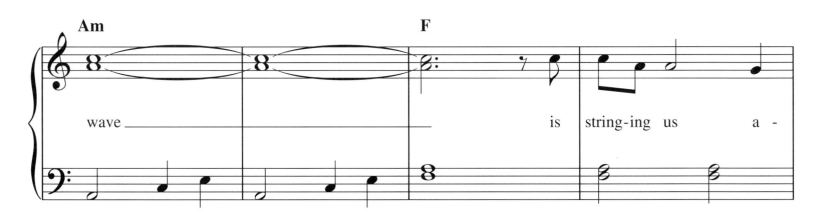

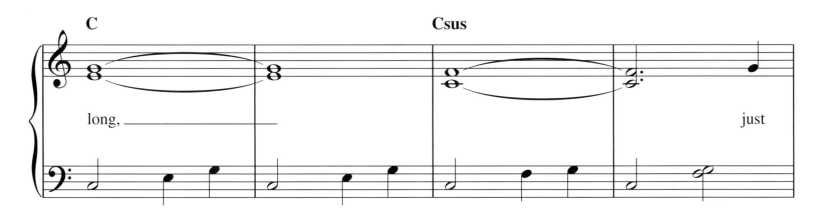

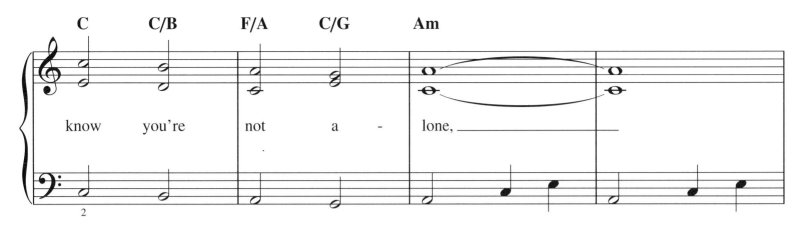

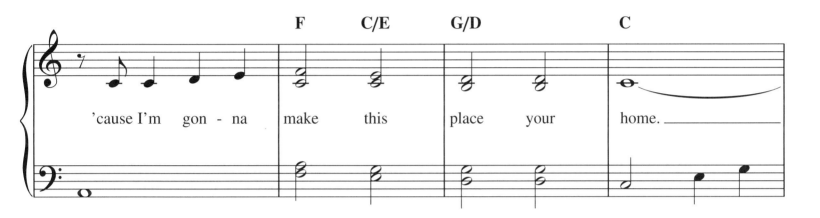

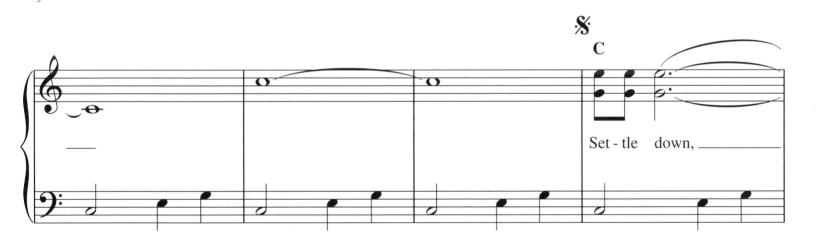

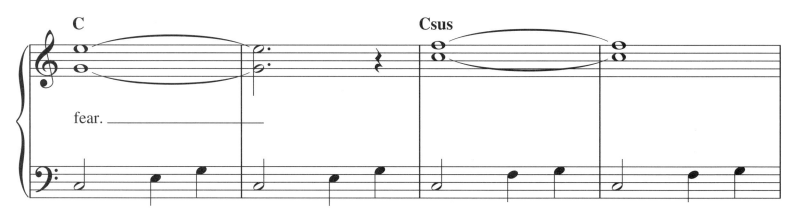

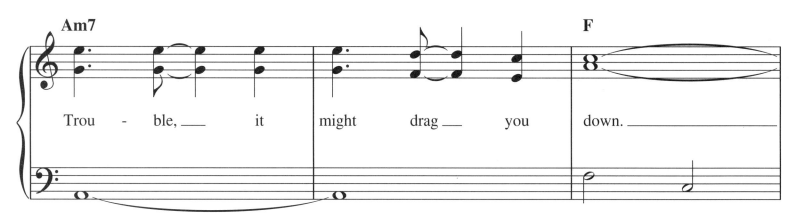

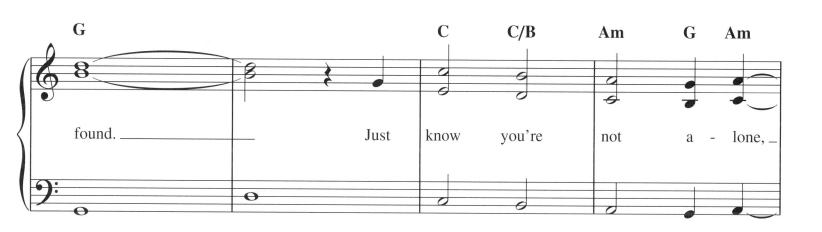

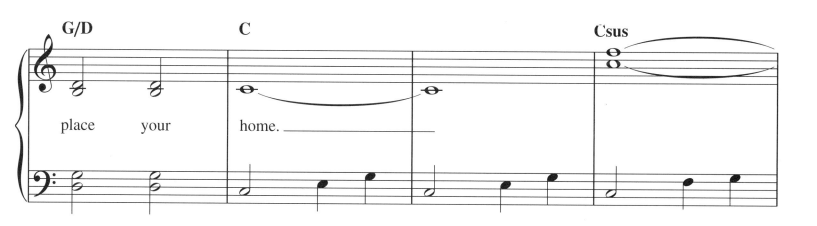

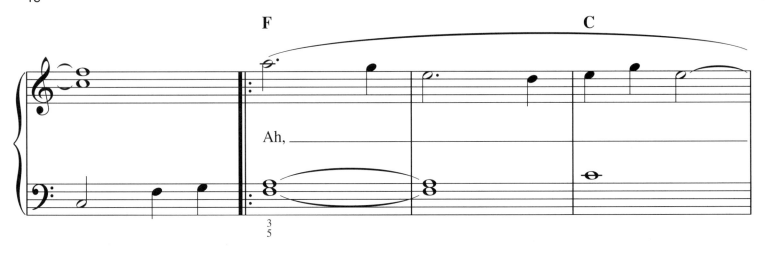

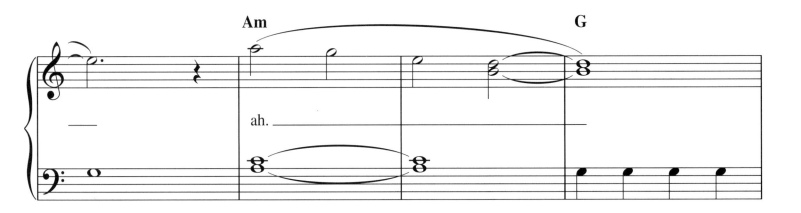

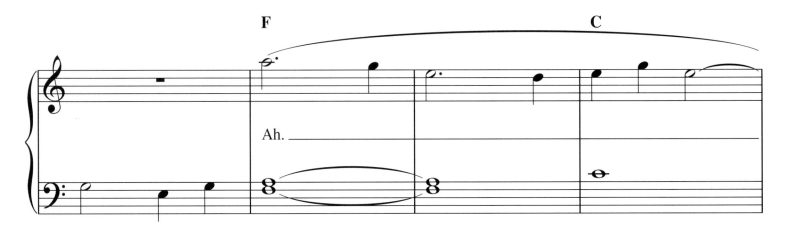

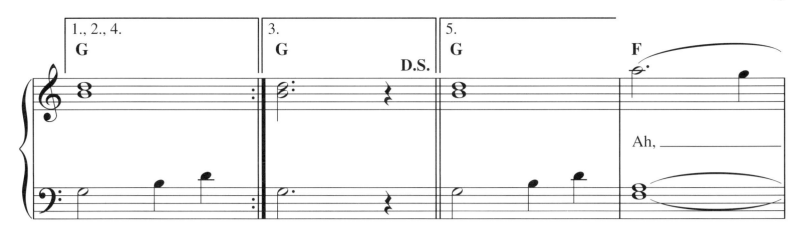

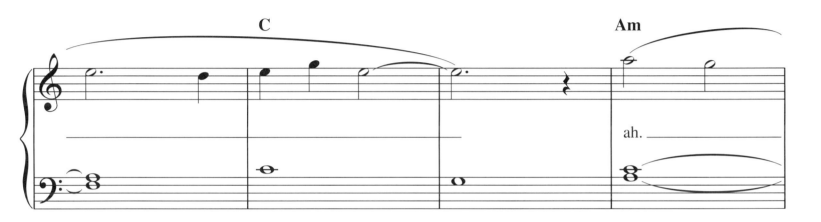

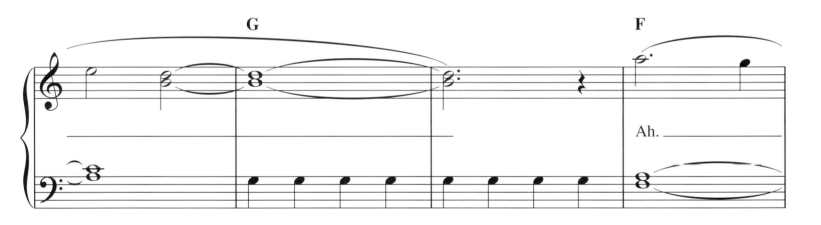

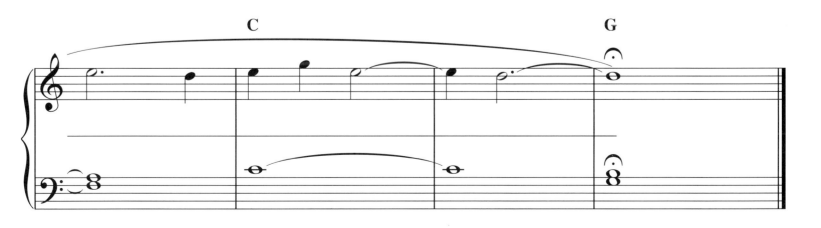

NEXT TO ME

Words and Music by EMELI SANDÉ,
HARRY CRAZE, HUGO CHEGWIN
and ANUP PAUL

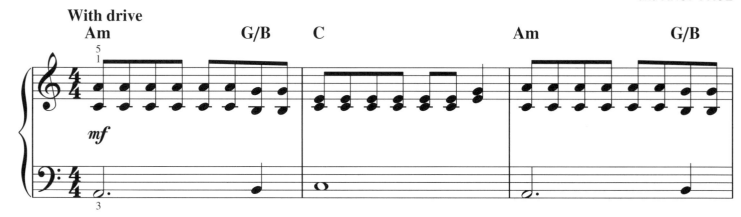

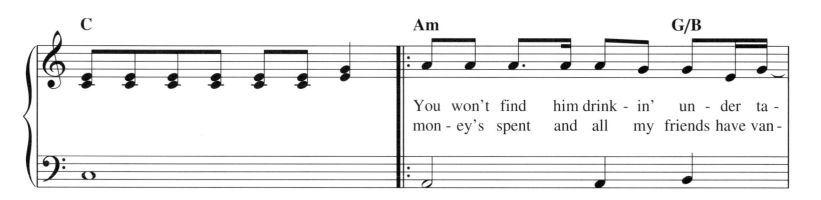

You won't find him drink - in' un - der ta -
mon - ey's spent and all my friends have van -

- bles,
- ished, and I can't

roll - in' dice and stay - in' out till
seem to find no help or love for

three.
free.

You won't ev - er find __ him bein' un -
I know there's no need __ for me to

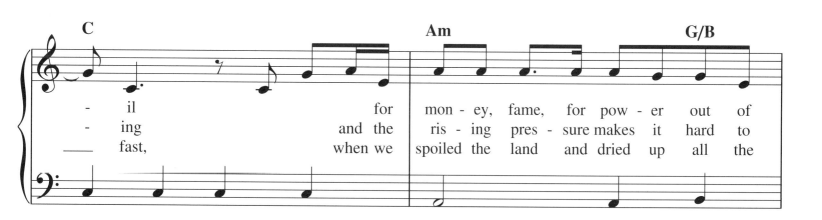

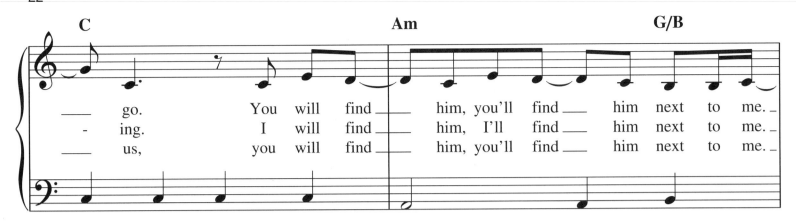

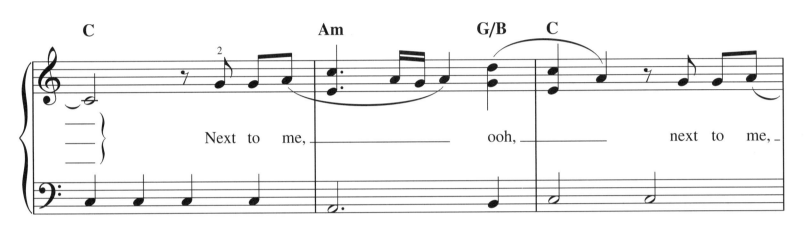

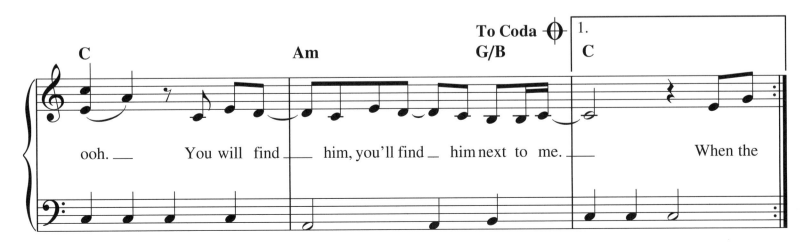

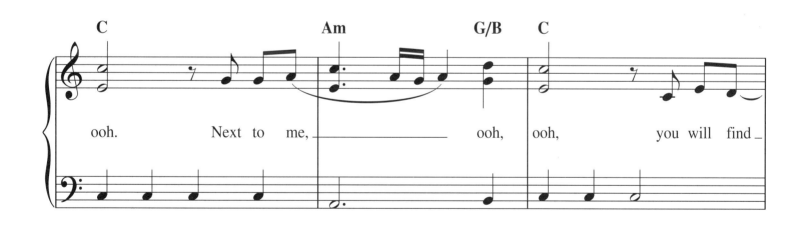

JUST GIVE ME A REASON

Words and Music by ALECIA MOORE,
JEFF BHASKER and NATE RUESS

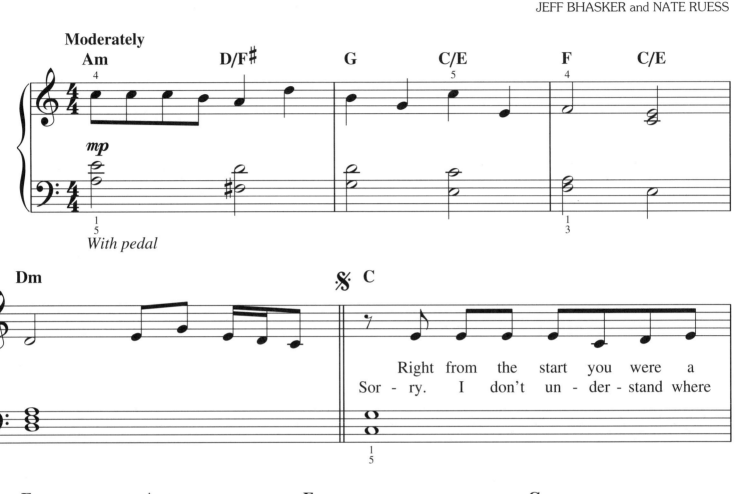

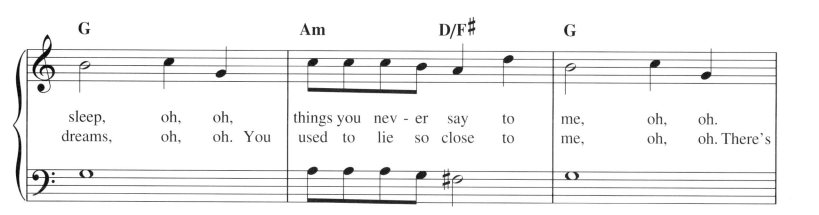

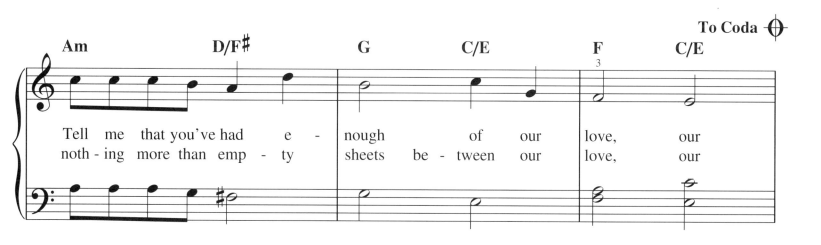

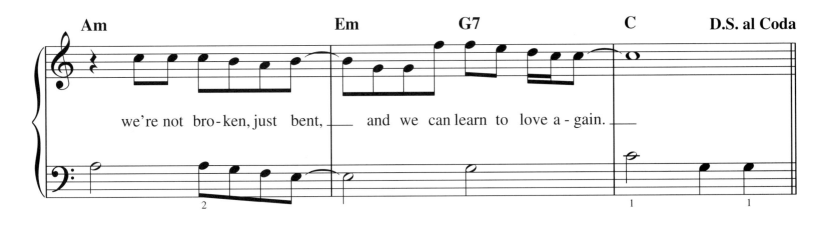

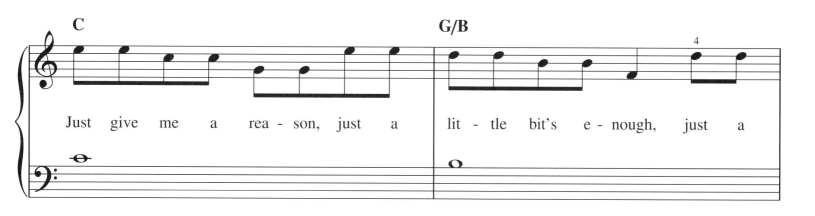

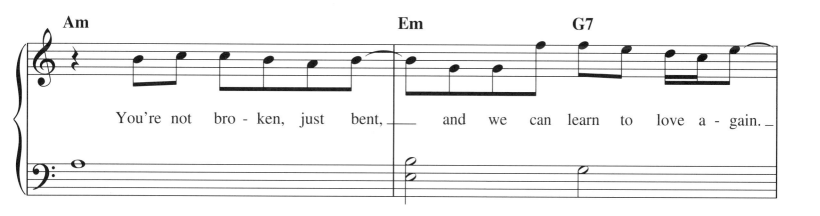

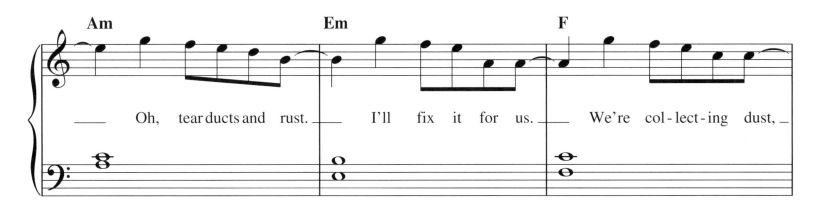

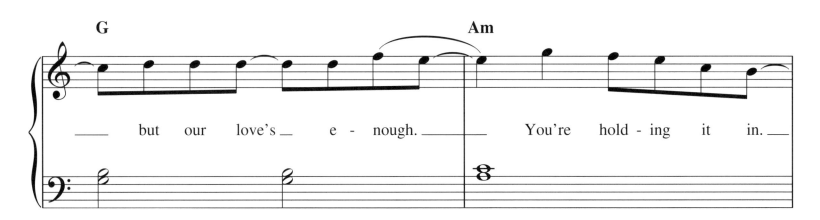

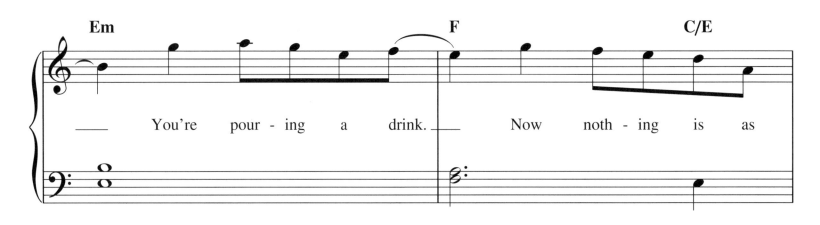

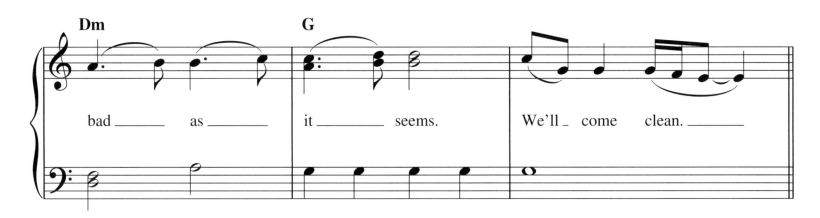

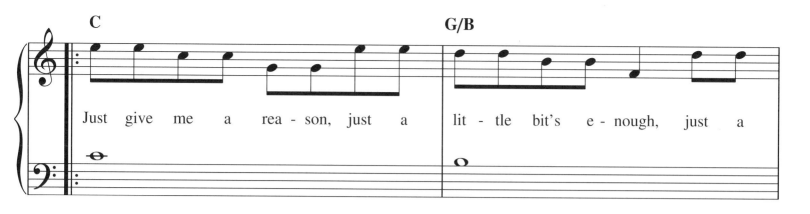

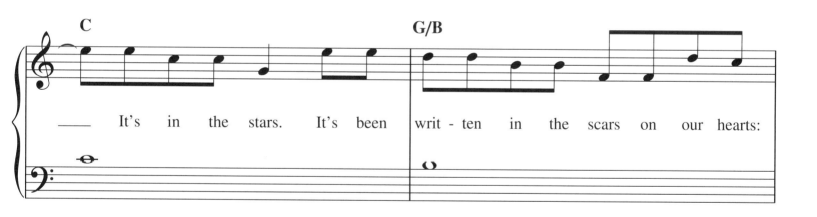

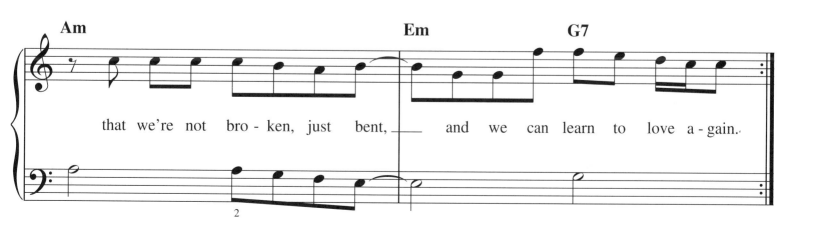

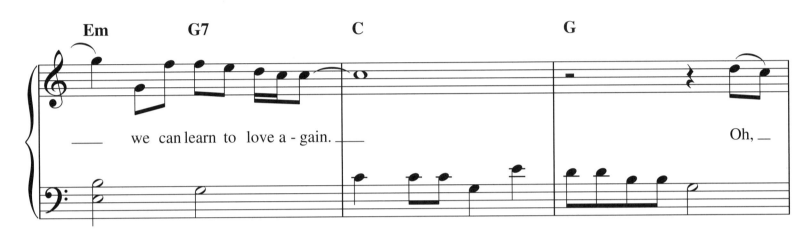

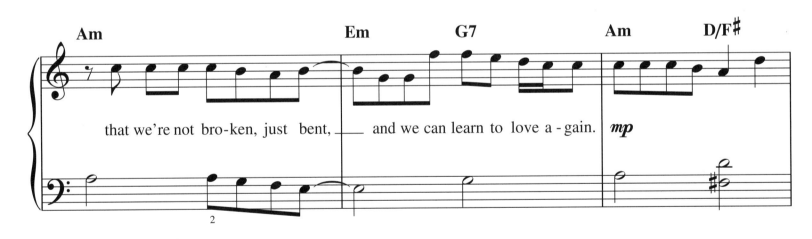

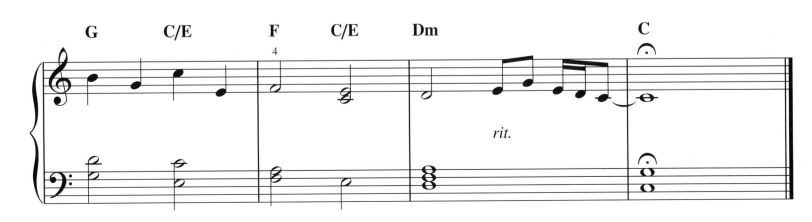

It's Easy to Play Your Favorite Songs with Hal Leonard Easy Piano Books

Beatles Best for Easy Piano
Easy arrangements of 120 Beatles hits. A truly remarkable collection including: All My Loving • And I Love Her • Come Together • Eleanor Rigby • Get Back • Help! • Hey Jude • I Want to Hold Your Hand • Let It Be • Michelle • many, many more.
00364092......................$24.99

The Best Broadway Songs Ever
The 2nd edition of this bestseller features 65+ Broadway faves: All I Ask of You • I Wanna Be a Producer • Just in Time • My Funny Valentine • On My Own • Seasons of Love • The Sound of Music • Tomorrow • Where or When • Younger Than Springtime • more!
00300178 ....$21.99

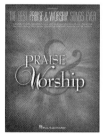

The Best Praise & Worship Songs Ever
The name says it all: over 70 of the best P&W songs today. Titles include: Awesome God • Blessed Be Your Name • Come, Now Is the Time to Worship • Days of Elijah • Here I Am to Worship • Open the Eyes of My Heart • Shout to the Lord • We Fall Down • and more.
00311312......................$19.99

The Best Songs Ever
Over 70 all-time favorite songs, including: All I Ask of You • Body and Soul • Call Me Irresponsible • Edelweiss • Fly Me to the Moon • The Girl from Ipanema • Here's That Rainy Day • Imagine • Let It Be • Moonlight in Vermont • People • Somewhere Out There • Tears in Heaven • Unforgettable • The Way We Were • and more.
00359223......................$19.95

Ten Top Hits for Easy Piano
Ten tunes from the top of the charts in 2006: Because of You • Black Horse and the Cherry Tree • Breaking Free • Jesus Take the Wheel • Listen to Your Heart • Over My Head (Cable Car) • The Riddle • Unwritten • Upside Down • You're Beautiful.
00310530......................$10.95

Jumbo Easy Piano Songbook
200 classical favorites, folk songs and jazz standards. Includes: Amazing Grace • Beale Street Blues • Bridal Chorus • Buffalo Gals • Canon in D • Cielito Lindo • Danny Boy • The Entertainer • Für Elise • Greensleeves • Jamaica Farewell • Marianne • Molly Malone • Ode to Joy • Peg O' My Heart • Rockin' Robin • Yankee Doodle • dozens more!
00311014......................$19.99

Best Children's Songs Ever
A great collection of over 100 songs, including: Alphabet Song • The Bare Necessities • Beauty and the Beast • Eensy Weensy Spider • The Farmer in the Dell • Hakuna Matata • My Favorite Things • Puff the Magic Dragon • The Rainbow Connection • Take Me Out to the Ball Game • Twinkle, Twinkle Little Star • Winnie the Pooh • and more.
00310360......................$19.95

150 of the Most Beautiful Songs Ever
Easy arrangements of 150 of the most popular songs of our time. Includes: Bewitched • Fly Me to the Moon • How Deep Is Your Love • My Funny Valentine • Some Enchanted Evening • Tears in Heaven • Till There Was You • Yesterday • You Are So Beautiful • and more. 550 pages of great music!
00311316......................$24.95

50 Easy Classical Themes
Easy arrangements of 50 classical tunes representing more than 30 composers, including: Bach, Beethoven, Chopin, Debussy, Dvorak, Handel, Haydn, Liszt, Mozart, Mussorgsky, Puccini, Rossini, Schubert, Strauss, Tchaikovsky, Vivaldi, and more.
00311215......................$12.95

Today's Country Hits
A collection of 13 contemporary country favorites, including: Bless the Broken Road • Jesus Take the Wheel • Summertime • Tonight I Wanna Cry • When I Get Where I'm Goin' • When the Stars Go Blue • and more.
00290188......................$12.95

VH1's 100 Greatest Songs of Rock and Roll
The results from the VH1 show that featured the 100 greatest rock and roll songs of all time are here in this awesome collection! Songs include: Born to Run • Good Vibrations • Hey Jude • Hotel California • Imagine • Light My Fire • Like a Rolling Stone • Respect • and more.
00311110......................$27.95

Disney's My First Song Book
16 favorite songs to sing and play. Every page is beautifully illustrated with full-color art from Disney features. Songs include: Beauty and the Beast • Bibbidi-Bobbidi-Boo • Circle of Life • Cruella De Vil • A Dream Is a Wish Your Heart Makes • Hakuna Matata • Under the Sea • Winnie the Pooh • You've Got a Friend in Me • and more.
00310322......................$16.99

HAL•LEONARD®
CORPORATION
7777 W. BLUEMOUND RD. P.O.BOX 13819 MILWAUKEE, WI 53213

0512

Hal Leonard
Piano White Pages

Modeled after our best-selling *Guitar Tab White Pages*, these books could be the best piano compilations ever!

Piano White Pages

200 songs, including: Amazed • Brown Eyed Girl • California Dreamin' • Clocks • Come Sail Away • Come to My Window • Dancing Queen • Do You Really Want to Hurt Me • Dust in the Wind • Easy • Fast Car • Free Bird • Good Vibrations • Happy Together • Hot Hot Hot • I Hope You Dance • I Will Remember You • I Will Survive • Jack and Diane • Landslide • Oops!...I Did It Again • Smooth • Tears in Heaven • These Boots Are Made for Walkin' • Time After Time • Walking in Memphis • Werewolves of London • You Can't Hurry Love • You've Got a Friend • You've Lost That Lovin' Feelin' • and many more.
00311276 P/V/G $29.99

Piano White Pages Volume 2

200 more songs, with no duplication from Volume 1! This volume includes: All by Myself • Annie's Song • At Seventeen • Autumn Leaves • Beyond the Sea • Blowin' in the Wind • Bridge over Troubled Water • Candle in the Wind • Don't Know Why • Don't Stop Believin' • Downtown • Hello Again • Hey Jude • I Will Always Love You • I Write the Songs • Longer • Lullaby of Birdland • Misty • Mona Lisa • Morning Has Broken • My Funny Valentine • My Way • Puttin' on the Ritz • The Rainbow Connection • Rumour Has It • Satin Doll • Someone like You • Time After Time • Up Where We Belong • We've Only Just Begun • Woman • You Are So Beautiful • You're the Inspiration • and more.
00312562 P/V/G $29.99

Prices, contents and availability subject to change without notice.

HAL•LEONARD®
CORPORATION

7777 W. BLUEMOUND RD. P.O. BOX 13819 MILWAUKEE, WI 53213

www.halleonard.com

Broadway Piano White Pages

The ultimate collection of every Broadway song you'll ever need – over 200 in all – arranged for piano and voice with guitar chord frames. This amazing folio features: All the Things You Are • And All That Jazz • Another Suitcase in Another Hall • Any Dream Will Do • Big Spender • Bring Him Home • Brotherhood of Man • Consider Yourself • Dancing on the Ceiling • Give My Regards to Broadway • I Am Changing • I Could Have Danced All Night • I Don't Know How to Love Him • On My Own • One • Seasons of Love • The Sound of Music • A Spoonful of Sugar • Tomorrow • We Go Together • and more. 896 pages!
00311500 P/V/G $29.99

Easy Piano White Pages

The largest collection of easy piano arrangements ever, with 200 songs and over 860 pages! Includes: Alison • Bennie and the Jets • Bridge over Troubled Water • California Girls • Crazy Little Thing Called Love • Don't Worry, Be Happy • Footloose • Hey, Soul Sister • I Get Around • If I Were a Carpenter • King of the Road • Layla • Maybe I'm Amazed • My Girl • Night Moves • Peter Gunn • Saving All My Love for You • Take Me Home, Country Roads • Walk This Way • You Are My Sunshine • and many, many more!
00312566 Easy Piano $29.99

The E-Z Play® Today White Pages

More than 330 hits in all styles fill 900 pages in the largest collection ever of songs in our world-famous notation! Features: All of Me • Big Spender • Brian's Song • Color My World • Come Fly with Me • Dancing Queen • Dream Weaver • Fly like an Eagle • The Godfather Theme • Guilty • Jackson • Lush Life • Monday, Monday • Moon River • Puppy Love • Rockin' Robin • Skylark • Tangerine • Truly • The Very Thought of You • Y.M.C.A. • You Raise Me Up • and scores more!
00100234 E-Z Play Today #316 .... $27.99